GEARED FOR GROWTH BIBLE STUDIES

THE WORLD'S ONLY HOPE

A STUDY IN LUKE'S GOSPEL

BIBLE STUDIES TO IMPACT THE LIVES OF ORDINARY PEOPLE

Christian Focus Publications

The Word Worldwide

Written by Dorothy Russell

Christian Focus Publications

publishes books for all ages

Our mission statement –

STAYING FAITHFUL
In dependence upon God we seek to help make His infallible word, the Bible, relevant. Our aim is to ensure that the Lord Jesus Christ is presented as the only hope to obtain forgiveness of sin, live a useful life and look forward to heaven with Him.

REACHING OUT
Christ's last command requires us to reach out to our world with His gospel. We seek to help fulfill that by publishing books that point people towards Jesus and help them develop a Christ-like maturity. We aim to equip all levels of readers for life, work, ministry and mission.

Books in our adult range are published in three imprints.
Christian Focus contains popular works including biographies, commentaries, basic doctrine, and Christian living. Our children's books are also published in this imprint.
Mentor focuses on books written at a level suitable for Bible College and seminary students, pastors, and other serious readers; the imprint includes commentaries, doctrinal studies, examination of current issues, and church history.
Christian Heritage contains classic writings from the past.

For details of our titles visit us on our website
www.christianfocus.com

ISBN 1-85792-886-5

Published in 2003 by
Christian Focus Publications, Geanies House,
Fearn, Ross-shire, IV20 ITW, Scotland
and
WEC International, Bulstrode, Oxford Road,
Gerrards Cross, Bucks, SL9 8SZ

Cover design by Alister MacInnes

Printed and bound by J W Arrowsmith, Bristol

CONTENTS

QUESTIONS AND NOTES

ANSWER GUIDE

PREFACE

GEARED FOR GROWTH

'Where there's LIFE there's GROWTH:
Where there's GROWTH there's LIFE.'

WHY GROW a study group?

Because as we study the Bible and share together we can

- learn to combat loneliness, depression, staleness, frustration, and other problems
- get to understand and love each other
- become responsive to the Holy Spirit's dealing and obedient to God's Word
                                                     and that's GROWTH.

How do you GROW a study group?

- Just start by asking a friend to join you and then aim at expanding your group.
- Study the set portions daily (they are brief and easy: no catches).
- Meet once a week to discuss what you find.
- Befriend others, both Christians and non Christians, and work away together
                                                     see how it GROWS!

WHEN you GROW ...

This will happen at school, at home, at work, at play, in your youth group, your student fellowship, women's meetings, mid-week meetings, churches and communities,
                                     you'll be REACHING THROUGH TEACHING

SOMETHING TO REMEMBER

Jesus said: 'The Holy Spirit will teach you all things,
and will remind you of everything I have said to you.'

PRAYER: Lord God, our Father, We have all had time to think about this week's passage at home on our own. Now I expect the Holy Spirit to teach me something special from these verses, and then to remind me of it from time to time.
I pray that my heart will be open to receive what He has to say. AMEN.

Each week, after you have shared together in your group, write below one particular truth you have learned from that part of Luke's Gospel.

STUDY 1
Communication – God to man.

STUDY 7
Giving up everything.

STUDY 2
Voices.

STUDY 8
Lost and found.

STUDY 3
The ring of authority.

STUDY 9
If you had been there ...

STUDY 4
The disciples at school.

STUDY 10
Head-on collisions.

STUDY 5
Following Jesus.

STUDY 11
'There was no other good enough ...'

STUDY 6
Teaching about the Kingdom.

STUDY 12
The end – and the beginning

INTRODUCTORY STUDY

If you were a Jew living in the first century, you would be very careful not to mix with certain people – indeed, you would avoid them at all costs! Who are these people?

I. **Gentiles** (anyone who is not a Jew). You would regard them as being irrevocably lost, outside the promises which God gave to Abraham, and therefore, beyond the scope of salvation.

2. **Samaritans.** These people were descendants of Jews who had intermarried with other nations. You would consider they deserved all the hatred and scorn that respectable Jews poured on them.

3. **Tax-collectors** and other immoral people. You would despise them and certainly never be seen in their company. They were real 'no-hopers'.

4. **The poor.** You would probably ignore them as they grovelled and begged in your pathway. You would pretend they didn't exist.

5. **Women** (presuming you are a man!). You would thank God daily, in public, that He had not made you a woman. And for a very good reason – they were definitely inferior second-class citizens.

Now Luke, living at that time, was a Gentile himself. He had spent much time in the company of the Apostle Paul, a Jew. You see, Paul's traditional Jewish attitude had been revolutionised when he came to know Jesus Christ. At his conversion, when God told him he was to carry the message of Jesus to the Gentiles, he was aghast! But as he was faithful to the task, he must have realised that this had been God's plan all along. So, when Luke wrote his gospel, he was careful to show that from the very beginning God planned that His message should be for all kinds and classes of people. Luke paints a portrait of Jesus as One whose love reaches out to every member of the human race.

See how he selects incidents to emphasise this, for example, in the following references;

Gentiles	2:28-32; 4:25-27; 7:2, 9.
Samaritans	9:51, 52; 10:30-35; 17:12-16.
Outcasts	7:36-39, 48; 18:13-14; 19:1-7, 23:42, 43.
Poor	12:33; 14:13; 16:19-23.
Women	8:1-3; 10:38, 39; 13:10-13.

So, if you had been a Jew, you might have been rather startled as you read Luke's account for the first time.

But let's face it! You are not a Jew living in the first century. What difference, then, does it make to us today, that Christ's offer of salvation is open to everyone, irrespective of birth or circumstances?

Discuss what kinds of people in your locality might be the parallels of those listed above.

How is the Christian community in your area trying to share the message of Jesus with these people? Do you think this is important? Are you involved on a personal level? Discuss this together.

* * *

Read Luke 1:1-4 in different versions. From these verses, discover:

To whom was Luke's Gospel addressed?
Was he the first to write such an account?
Where did he get his information?
What was his attitude to the task?
What was his purpose in writing?

* * *

Discuss:

How do you think Luke's 'orderly account' can help people today?
Why do you think Luke didn't simply write a biography of Jesus?
What do you expect to gain personally from the study of this book?

Michael Wilcock in his book, THE MESSAGE OF LUKE, The Saviour of the World (Pub. IVP – a splendid book), comments on the first four verses of Luke:

'It should whet our appetite, especially if we have become too accustomed to living on spiritual snacks, to know what pains Luke has taken to prepare this feast. It consists, basically, of the living facts which were common to all the early 'Gospels', but it has been carefully prepared, supplemented with extra courses, and attractively served. We owe it more than a perfunctory nibble.'

STUDY 1
COMMUNICATION – GOD TO MAN

QUESTIONS

DAY 1 *Malachi 4:5-6; Luke 1:5-25.*
a) What things did the angel tell Zechariah about the son that would be born to him and his wife?
b) What happened to Zechariah because he did not believe the message from God?

DAY 2 *Isaiah 7:14; Luke 1:26-38.*
a) What things did the angel tell Mary about the Son that would be born to her?
b) What explanation was given of how this Child could be born to a girl who was a virgin?
c) What was Mary's reaction to the news?

DAY 3 *I Samuel 2:1, 2, 5, 7; Luke 1:39-56.*
a) What happened to Elizabeth when she heard Mary's voice?
b) In Mary's song, what does she say about God's mercy and God's power?

DAY 4 *Luke 1:57-80.*
a) What are we told about Zechariah in verses 63-67?
b) For whom does Zechariah praise God in verses 68-75?
c) To whom do verses 76 and 77 refer?

DAY 5 *Luke 2:1-20; Galatians 4:4-5.*
a) Read these well-known verses prayerfully several times. What impresses you most about them?
b) Read Matthew 1:20-23. Who, in fact, broke into history that night?

DAY 6 *Luke 2:21-40.*
a) What do we read about the Holy Spirit in verses 25-27?
b) Verse 33 – what do you think amazed Mary and Joseph so much in what Simeon had said?

DAY 7 *Luke 2:41-52; John 4:34.*
a) What was the boy Jesus doing in the Temple?
b) What did Jesus' answer to His mother's question show?

NOTES

Imagine Dr. Luke as he sits down to write. He has collected a wealth of information, some from the apostles, some from other eye-witnesses, some from Mary, the mother of Jesus. He ponders ... what to include, and what to leave out?

He wants to make it clear that Jesus was:

- the One for whom all sincere Jews had been waiting so long,
- the One who came from God,
- the One who would save His people from their sins.

He thinks for a little longer, prays, picks up his quill and inspired by the Holy Spirit begins to write ...

Zechariah and Elizabeth had been faithfully praying for the coming of a Saviour to their nation. For 400 years even the voice of prophecy had been silent, and this couple must have had great faith to continue all their lives believing that God would do what He had promised, and send a Saviour. So, the first exciting GOOD NEWS is that God is about to send a messenger to tell everyone that the Saviour is coming soon, and the surprise is that they themselves will be the parents of this man!

Mary next receives some astounding news. It is no ordinary child who is to be born to her, and in no ordinary way – but God Himself, coming to planet Earth, bringing Salvation to all mankind. His Name? 'Jesus' – 'the Lord is Salvation.'

In Mary's song she has a vision of what this coming Salvation will mean, nothing less than a revolution in man's thinking and attitudes. Indeed, God has already begun this revolution by choosing 'what the world looks down on and despises, and thinks is nothing ...' (I Cor. 1:28) to bring about His wonderful purposes. And God breaking into history will continue to turn things upside down and show man a completely different set of values.

Zechariah, inspired by the Holy Spirit, then prophesies that Jesus will save His people from their enemies – but goes on to note that true Salvation means to be saved from spiritual enemies, i.e. having one's sins forgiven. So the wonderful GOOD NEWS that Zechariah rejoices in, is that Jesus has come to save His people from their sins.

* * *

The actual happening of Jesus' birth was, of course, of the greatest importance, but it is the Word of God concerning this event that Luke highlights so that we may know its significance.

The word of God came first *through an angel* to the shepherds.

The message:

> 'The babe that has been born is –
> Saviour' (the One who alone can bring Salvation),
> Christ (God's promised Messiah)
> and Lord (God Himself).

Notice that the shepherds passed on the divine message to Mary and Joseph as well as to others that they met; notice, also, that Mary hid this word of God in her heart and thought deeply about it.

A week later, the word of God came *through a prophet*, Simeon, and the revelation this time was that the Child would be – 'A light to reveal God's will to the Gentiles.'

Mary and Joseph were amazed at this word of prophecy and could only marvel at the unexpected purposes of God. Who would ever have thought at that time, that God's saving love would reach out to the Gentiles?

After 12 years, the Word of God came *through the boy Jesus* who was Himself, 'the Word made flesh' (John 1:14). What revelation did these first recorded words from His lips bring?

'My Father,' He said, meaning God not Joseph.

He also showed (as He later said) that His work was to do his Father's work which was to bring Salvation to man. Although Mary did not understand His reply at the time, she treasured these things, too, in her heart.

So, Luke takes us back 'to the beginning', and gives us not only the facts, but the Divine explanation from the mouth of God to help us understand them.

* * *

'My Son,
Farewell.
A body I've prepared
for you
in Mary
Jewish girl
betrothed to Joseph
Jewish carpenter.
You who have been with me
from everlasting days
who with me made all things
including earth and man
and Mary
tonight become
a creature vulnerable
baby most helpless.
The swirling cloud
takes you to her
through darkest night.

I send an angel army
to protect,
proclaim your birth.
You'll grow
and spend a few days' light
then darkest noon
and you'll return.
I'll have the dust of earth
the virgin's fruit
at my right hand
for evermore.
Tonight I joy
that you delight to do my will
take God-sized step
to earth and womb
and tree.
My Son, Farewell
I hear a baby's cry.'

('Christmas voices' by Joseph Bayley.
Reprinted from Decision magazine).

* * *

Each person should now fill in the blank space on page 5 for this study.

STUDY 2

VOICES

QUESTIONS

DAY 1   *Isaiah 40:3-5; Luke 3:1-6, 18.*
a) What made John decide to start preaching?
b) How did John describe himself?
c) What part did he play in God's plan?

DAY 2   *Luke 3:7-20; 7:29, 30.*
a) What was John's message to: the Jews in general (v. 8)? the people in verse 11? the tax-collectors? the soldiers?
b) If you met John the Baptist today, what particular message might he have for you?

DAY 3   *Matthew 3:13-15; Luke 3:21, 22; 1 John 3:5.*
a) Look at Luke 3:3 again. Why do you think Jesus asked to be baptised?
b) The voice from heaven quoted parts of Psalm 2:7 and Isaiah 42:1-3. How are these verses a good picture of Jesus?

DAY 4   *Luke 3:23 (and skim through to the end of the chapter!)*
a) Why do you think Luke included this family tree here?
b) Compare 3:31 (David) with 1:32; and 3:34 (Abraham) with 1:55. The genealogy is traced back to Adam. What important distinction is made in Romans 5:17 between Adam and Jesus?

DAY 5   *Luke 4:1-13.*
a) Why do you think the devil tempted Jesus to turn the stones into bread?
b) How did Jesus answer the devil's temptations?
c) What can we learn from this?

DAY 6   *Luke 4:14-30.*
a) What did Jesus claim about Himself in verse 21?
b) What made the people so furious in verses 28 and 29 (glance back to our Introductory Study)?

DAY 7   a) What do we read about the Holy Spirit in the following verses: Luke 1:35; 3:16, 22; 4:1, 14, 18?
b) How many verses can you find in this week's study which tell us something about whose son Jesus was?

LUKE • STUDY 2 • VOICES . . . .

11

NOTES

They are all around us all the time. Voices. Voices of encouragement ... criticism ... friendship ... loneliness ... happiness ... fear.

Voices which shout, 'Come on! Everybody's doing it – it must be okay.'

Voices which whisper, 'The right way isn't easy, but it's best in the end.'

Luke is telling us about voices, too. Important voices, deceiving voices – and the voices of God and His Son.

1. *A voice in the desert*
'The King is coming. Get ready!'
'How?'
'By a change of heart.'
'We don't need that. We are Abraham's descendants.'
'Don't think your religious heritage will save you.'
'Why?'
'Because only your lifestyle will show whether you have had a change of heart or not.'
'What are we to do then?'
'Turn away from your sins and ask God to forgive you.'
Have you heard this voice? Have you listened to it carefully?
It could make all the difference to where you spend eternity.
It's important.

2. *A voice from heaven*
Jesus had been praying (perhaps about God's will for Him?). And the Father answered. The Voice linked together two Old Testament prophecies – one about God's Son, and one about God's Special Servant.

What did it mean to be God's own dear Son? It meant to be a Servant. It meant a life of joyful obedience, service, and suffering ... unto death.

Later, Jesus said, 'Anyone who wants to follow Me, must put aside his own desires and conveniences, and carry his cross with him every day, and keep close to Me.' (Luke 9:23 – Living Bible).

3. *The voice of the devil*
He had three suggestions to make:

Suggestion 1
Provide for man's physical needs popularity.

Jesus' Alternative
Satisfy man's deepest needs even though it and win means rejection.

Suggestion 2
Bring political deliverance and be hailed as a Champion.

His work is to deliver men from the power of the devil.

Suggestion 3
Throw yourself down physically and prove that God will protect you. Do a spectacular miracle to convince everyone.

Jesus would indeed go down to the depths, even to where He would cry, 'My God, why have you forsaken Me?' But in secret and in silence, His Father would 'bear Him up' as He had promised.

The voice of the devil offered the easy way to satisfaction – a 'do-it-yourself', 'get-rich-quick', 'instant success' idea. But the froth and bubble would soon fizzle out and be finished. Jesus chose God's path of sacrifice, and the guarantee said, 'Eternal reward.'
The devil's offers to you are very tempting! But don't listen to him.

4. *The voice of Jesus*
'You who are spiritually poor, I have good news for you!
You who are in Satan's clutches, I've come to set you free.
You who are blind to the wonder and beauty of life lived to the full, I've come to show you what it's like.
You who are cut off from God by sin, I've come to rescue you.
And these gifts are for any who will take them.'

Did you hear that? It's almost too good to be true. But it is true, for the words are spoken by Truth Himself.

5. *The voices of ignorance and anger*
'Who is He, anyway?'
'We can't believe He's anything special.'
'We're quite all right as we are, thanks.'
'We don't need Jesus. We don't want Jesus.
'He makes us feel uncomfortable.'
'Let's get rid of Him.'
And we hear the echo, 'Crucify! Crucify!'
Can you hear these voices today? Sadly, they are everywhere. Be careful to whom you listen because you are responsible for your choice!

* * *

What has the Holy Spirit taught you today? Take time to write it on page 5.

STUDY 3
THE RING OF AUTHORITY

QUESTIONS

DAY 1   *Luke 4:31-44.*
a) What were the people so amazed at in verses 22, 32 and 36? (See also Mark 1:22.)
b) How did Jesus heal the people mentioned in verses 35, 39 and 41?
c) What was the work that He had to do at this time?

DAY 2   *Luke 5:1-11.*
a) Why had the people come to the lake shore?
b) What made Peter do what he, a seasoned fisherman, considered ridiculous?
c) How does Jesus affect your everyday occupation?

DAY 3   *Leviticus 13:45-46; Luke 5:12-26.*
a) Why was Jesus' touch so unexpected and so important to the man in Luke 5 verse 12?
b) What amazed and frightened the people most about the healing of the paralysed man?

DAY 4   *Luke 5:27-39.*
a) For what two reasons was Jesus criticized?
b) In His replies, whom did He say He was like? and why?

DAY 5   *Luke 6:1-11.*
a) What is Jesus demonstrating here about the Sabbath?
b) How can Matthew 22:36-40 help us to decide what to do (or not to do) on the Lord's Day?

DAY 6   *Matthew 19:28; Luke 6:12-26; Ephesians 2:20.*
a) What did Jesus do before choosing the twelve?
b) What three groups of people are mentioned in Luke 6 verse 17?
c) What should be our first priorities, according to verses 20-26 of Luke 6?

DAY 7   *Luke 6:27-49.*
a) Discuss whether it is 1) possible or 2) practical to live as suggested in verses 27-38.
b) What kind of person is the man like who built his house on a rock?
c) How does this apply to the verses you have been discussing?

NOTES

In the first section of this week's study (4:31–5:39), Luke gives us a series of stories which illustrate the authority that Jesus had. Notice the power of His WORD.

'Listen!' says Luke, 'when the Son of God speaks:

1. 'He challenges men's minds'
How fortunate were those people in Galilee, to sit under such a magnificent preacher! Yet even today, where that same Word of God is faithfully preached, people are amazed, impressed and challenged – because it comes with the same power, and is backed by the same authority.

2. 'He heals men's bodies'
Remember that Jesus didn't heal every sick person in the land, although it was in His power to do so. Notice also, that many who saw His miracles and knew they were for real, still didn't believe in Him as the Son of God. His miracles were always related to His teaching, and through them He demonstrated a particular truth to the men who saw them.

3. 'He changes men's lives'
When Jesus spoke to Peter in the boat Peter couldn't see any sense in doing what He asked. Yet the authority of His word was such that Peter replied, 'if you say so, I will let down the nets.' The result was overwhelming – but it wasn't the amount of fish that made Peter react the way he did, it was Jesus' supernatural power which scared him. Jesus, however, had deliberately performed this miracle to show His disciples that His power would draw men into the Kingdom. Their part was to commit themselves to Him and leave the old ways behind.

4. 'He heals broken relationships'
Lepers were not only outcasts from society, but also cut off from any fellowship with God's people, as leprosy was considered a sign of moral uncleanness. The Jews taught that only God could heal leprosy (see 2 Kgs 5:7), so this man's plea showed that he recognised Jesus as divine. Jesus' touch indicated that no-one was beyond reach of His love.

5. 'He forgives sin'
Luke has arranged these incidents in an ever-increasing order of importance. Here is the climax. 'God is the only One Who can forgive sins,' said the Pharisees. How true! At the word of Jesus, this man's sinful past was wiped out, and his life made new and clean. Is this even more important than healing the body?

'No question about that' says Jesus.
Do you really agree?
Does the Son of God speak today?
Does His Word still have authority?
Have you experienced any of the five points listed above?

* * *

In the second section of our study (Ch. 6), Luke shows that Jesus spoke with authority on: the Sabbath, the family of God, the Law.

Before Christianity or even Judaism existed, God instituted the Sabbath principle. He 'rested'. Man needs one day's rest in seven – a time of joyous fellowship with his Maker. But man fell into sin and broke that fellowship.

THE SABBATH

Thousands of years later, God again gave the Sabbath idea to His people through Moses, 'the seventh day is a day of rest dedicated to Me' (Exod. 20:10). Sadly, this became distorted.

Now Jesus deliberately brings to people's notice the fact that the Sabbath was not being kept as it should be. It was given for love, caring, and joyous fellowship with God – not for a burden, trying to keep man-made rules.

THE FAMILY OF GOD

The first family was created so that people could have fellowship with each other, to love and enjoy each other. Sin spoilt this too, when Cain murdered his brother.

As the whole world became increasingly wicked, God intervened and made a fresh start. He called first Abraham, and then the 12 tribes of Israel, to start a God-centred family. This also went wrong.

Now Jesus sets up a new family of God, and He chooses 12 men to be the foundation stones of His Church.

THE LAW

God gave Adam a law for living, at the very beginning. He told him what he was allowed to do and what he was not to do. We all know what happened.

Moses, in his day, received God's law written on stone, and once again people were told how God wanted them to live. But over the years this turned into bondage to a set of rules.

Jesus gives the royal law of love, self-denial and humility, and He lives it out in His own perfect life. Happiness, He says, will come from obeying this law.

* * *

Have you learned something new?
Write it in on page 5 to help you remember.

STUDY 4
THE DISCIPLES AT SCHOOL

QUESTIONS

DAY 1 *Luke 7:1-10.*
a) What impressed the Roman officer about Jesus?
b) This story shows Jesus' power over ... what?
c) What surprised Jesus about this man?

DAY 2 *Luke 7:11-17.*
a) Imagine the situation. Why would death have been so unusually tragic here?
b) This story shows Jesus' power over ... what?
c) What two reactions did the people have?

DAY 3 *Isaiah 29:18, 19; Matthew 11:2, 3; Luke 7:18-35.*
a) What did John the Baptist expect Jesus to do (Luke 3:16, 17)?
b) What can you find out from these verses about the Kingdom of God?

DAY 4 *Luke 7:36-50; 1 John 1:9.*
a) How does this incident enlarge upon Luke 7 verses 29 and 30 (that we read yesterday)?
b) This story shows Jesus' power over ... what?
c) Have you been forgiven much or little? How do you show your love for Jesus?

DAY 5 *Luke 8:1-21.*
a) Who went with Jesus on His preaching tour? What did they learn (v. 10)?
b) What does the parable of the sower highlight?
c) How does Jesus describe those who hear His Word and obey it?

DAY 6 *Luke 8:22-39.*
a) What do you think the disciples learned from the storm incident?
b) How would you have felt if you had been with Jesus when He got out of the boat?
c) If we are really frightened at any time, what should we remember?

DAY 7 *Luke 8:40-56.*
a) Why do you think Jesus wanted the sick woman to come out into the open?
b) How many people went into the room where the girl lay?
c) What might the three disciples have learned from what happened?

NOTES

Did you notice this about the stories in last week's study – we had to push our way through crowds of people to get near Jesus? At the beginning of His ministry, Jesus showed His power to the world at large:

> He healed in the synagogue, in front of all the worshippers. He healed great crowds at Peter's house. He was mobbed by the people even when He wanted to be alone. After the healing of the leper great crowds came to Him. He taught in a house so crowded that the only way in was by the roof!

Luke demonstrates this clearly as he writes.

Then he tells about the NEW ISRAEL being instituted – remember? A new Sabbath, a new family of God, a new Law. From among the great masses of people all around Him, Jesus began to call out His Church. (The word 'church' means just that 'called out').

* * *

Now, in chapter 7, Luke seems to zero in on Jesus with individuals, as he presents Jesus as King of the Kingdom – the Kingdom which is for those who recognise that they are poor and needy, and are willing to take what Jesus offers. The Kingdom which is available to every kind of person (remember our Introductory Study?).

So, we have the stories of:

the Gentile soldier – faith greater than any of the Jews;
the widow – heartbroken and needy;
John the Baptist – discouraged and doubting;
the prostitute – with many sins to be forgiven.

In the parable of the sower, which Luke places next, the message is underlined: only those who are receptive to the Word of God will be blessed by it. It is not your nationality, rank, or position that matters.

* * *

LESSONS FOR THE DISCIPLES – the 'called out' ones, the first members of His Church. Shouldn't we look closely at these lessons if we, too, have been 'called out' as members of His Church?

Let's see again what happened.

> 'One day Jesus got into a boat with His disciples (Luke 8:22) ... Jesus and His disciples sailed on (v. 26) ... as Jesus stepped ashore He was met by a man (v. 27) ... Jesus got into the boat and left (v. 37) ... When Jesus returned ... they had all been waiting for Him (v.40)

... then a man named Jairus arrived (v. 41) ... As Jesus went along (v. 42) ... a woman touched the edge of His cloak (v. 44) ... when He arrived at the house (v. 51) ....'

What a day! What a chain of events!

And it was Jesus who took the disciples across the lake, where the storm would be. He brought them to shore where the demon-possessed man was. He took them back to Capernaum, where Jairus was, drew attention to the sick woman, and took them into the room with the dead girl.

What lessons did they learn? Can we learn them too?

1. As followers of Jesus, we are not isolated from suffering.
2. We, ourselves, are powerless against danger, mental or physical illness, or death.
3. Jesus, alone can control evil in its various forms.
4. We need to stay close to Jesus, whatever happens.
5. We can trust Him to bring good out of evil – maybe not in the way we expect, but in His way.
6. 'In all these things we are more than conquerors through Him who loved us' (Rom. 8:37).

* * *

Remember to fill in the space on page 5 for Study 4.

LUKE • STUDY 4 • THE DISCIPLES AT SCHOOL • • • • • • •

STUDY 5
FOLLOWING JESUS

QUESTIONS

DAY 1   *Luke 9:1-17.*
a) What tasks were the disciples given to do in verses 1-6?
b) How were they able to do them?
c) Discuss the suggestions given by the disciples in verse 12 and by Jesus in verse 13.

DAY 2   *Luke 9:18-36; Galatians 2:19, 20.*
a) What did Peter realise about Jesus (Luke 9:18-20)?
b) What did Jesus tell them about Himself (vv. 21-27)?
c) What did the voice from heaven say about Him (vv. 28-36)?

DAY 3   *Luke 9:37-50.*
a) What do verses 40, 45, 46, 49 show us about the disciples?
b) In what ways do you sometimes feel inadequate?

DAY 4   *Luke 9:51-62.*
a) What shows us that James and John had forgotten Jesus' teaching in chapter 6:27?
b) Put in your own words what Jesus was saying to those who said they wanted to follow Him. Read also 1 Peter 1:6-7.

DAY 5   *Luke 10:1-12.*
Jesus told the 72 (or 70) disciples: *Pray* ... what? *Go* ... where? *Stay* ... where? *Heal* ... whom? *Say* ... what?

DAY 6   *Luke 10:13-24.*
a) What made those disciples happy?
b) What did Jesus say should make us happy?
c) What made Jesus happy?

DAY 7   *Luke 10:25-42; John 4:9.*
a) What do you see as the main point of the story in Luke 10 verses 25-35?
b) What can we learn from the incident about Martha and Mary?

NOTES

Let's see what Chapter 9 has to tell us about following Jesus.

The Twelve
They were practising 'being Jesus' to others, not in their own strength, but with His power and authority. Because they stayed close to Him, He was able to involve them in the miracle of feeding the crowd. He provided what was needed, they gave it to the people.

Peter
Jesus knew His followers had to know for sure who He was. Peter was the first to stake everything on this. Herod, idly curious, stands in sharp contrast to Peter, and typifies those who don't want to get involved.

The way is not easy
For Jesus, it was a literal cross – and more. For His followers, it is crucifying self daily, giving up even relationships, if necessary, and committing their lives totally to Him.
  It is such a hard way that God Himself must give the needed strength:

To Jesus – the conversation with Moses and Elijah encouraged Him as He approached the cross,
To His followers – the Voice said, 'Yes, you're right. This is my Son, now listen to what He says.'

His followers may –

... have little faith.
The disciples had recently returned from a mission where they had healed and cast out demons. Why, then, could they not help this boy? They still had a lot to learn.

... or be stubborn.
Again, Jesus told them what was going to happen. But they didn't want to believe it, it was too unpleasant. They still had a lot to learn.

... or childish.
'Me first ...' 'I want to be at the top ...'
Oh dear, haven't they learned anything yet? Have you?

... or revengeful.
'James, when will you learn not to hit back?'
'John, do good to those who hate you.'
'Perhaps we need more time together, friends.'

And what can we learn from Chapter 10?

FOLLOWING JESUS involves spreading the Good News.
We should be like the 72 who were sent out. We don't need to be super-men and women. It is our message which is 'super', and the fact that Jesus has sent us. He has given us the authority.
    To whom can you talk about Jesus this week?

FOLLOWING JESUS involves caring for others to a degree that is, humanly speaking, unthinkable – like the Good Samaritan. Imagine the characters in this story coming from two violently opposed groups of people that you can think of, and one stopping to love and care for the other. It's impossible! Yet, this is what Jesus requires of His followers: that we love our enemies.

Where is that Christ-like love that makes a man
Forget himself,
Thinking only of what he can do
For others,
Loving his neighbour
As himself?
There are people here who have no neighbours!
They isolate themselves.
They do not love as You would, Lord,
They do not love!
There are people here who claim to love You, Lord.
They pray,
They praise,
They offer themselves to You.
They whisper and gossip about their fellow men,
They say they love You, but they do not love
Their brothers.
They do not love.   Russ Tyson.

FOLLOWING JESUS involves spending time alone with Him.
It is not that daily duties and routine work are wrong, but it is of the utmost importance that you and I take time daily to read His Word (i.e. listen to His teaching) and pray.
    Are you doing your questions every day – for a start?

Don't forget to write in 'something special' on page 5.

STUDY 6
TEACHING ABOUT THE KINGDOM

QUESTIONS

DAY 1 *Luke 11:1-13.*
a) What do these verses tell us about God?
b) What guidelines for prayer can you discover?

DAY 2 *Luke 11:14-26.*
a) Who do the 'strong man' and the 'someone stronger' represent?
b) From Acts 26:18 and 1 John 3:8 discover why Jesus came to our world.

DAY 3 *Matthew 12:39-40; Luke 11:16, 27-36.*
a) What was to be the 'sign' for the people of Jesus' day?
b) For what was the Queen of the South (Sheba) commended?

DAY 4 *Luke 11:37–12:3.*
a) Give two examples of how the Pharisees and teachers of the Law outwardly seemed very good, but inwardly were not.
b) How should we live, in the light of chapter 12:2, 3 and Hebrews 4:13?

DAY 5 *Luke 12:4-12.*
a) What solemn warnings are given in verses 5 and 10?
b) Look up how verses 11 and 12 were fulfilled in the days of the early Church: Acts 4:13 and 2 Timothy 4:16-18.

DAY 6 *Luke 12:13-34.*
a) In what practical ways can you and I follow the command of Jesus in verse 15?
b) What does Jesus mean by 'riches in heaven'? How do they differ from 'riches on earth'?

DAY 7 *Luke 12:35-59.*
a) We know that Jesus will return. What effect should this have on the way we live (2 Pet. 3:10-13)?
b) Take a few minutes to think prayerfully about the way you are living, remembering that the Lord may return at any time.

NOTES

Jesus said, 'I must preach the good news about the Kingdom of God.' And it is recorded that He went about bringing the good news of the Kingdom of God. What, then, is meant by 'the Kingdom of God'? Surely it is important for us to have this clear in our minds. Ever since Adam disobeyed God and sin entered the world, the kingdom of Satan has held sway.

Now Jesus has broken into Satan's domain, setting some of his captives free, driving out demons.

'The strong man', Satan, has been attacked by 'the stronger Man'. 'And this proves,' says Jesus, 'that the Kingdom of God has already come to you.' Obviously another kingdom has declared war on Satan's kingdom.

* * *

The meaning of the words, 'The kingdom of God is within you' (Luke 17:21) has been the subject of some discussion. But scholars generally agree that a better translation is, 'The Kingdom of God is among you', i.e. it is present in the Person and ministry of Jesus (see Tyndale Commentary p. 259). The secret of belonging to the Kingdom, therefore, lies in belonging to Jesus (Matt. 7:21-23).

The question is therefore asked, 'Is the Church the Kingdom of God?'

H. Ridderbos, in the New Bible Dictionary, writes: 'A connection exists between Kingdom and Church, but they are not identical, even in the present age. The Kingdom is the whole of God's redeeming activity in Christ in this world; the Church is the assembly of those who belong to Jesus Christ. The Church is the assembly of those ... in whose life the Kingdom takes visible form; ... she is also the community of those who wait for the coming of the Kingdom in glory.'

* * *

Jesus asked, 'What is the Kingdom of God like? What shall I compare it to?' Then He gave some parables to help us understand more about it. Matthew 13 has a collection of these together:

The Weeds
The farmer let the wheat (i.e. the people in the Kingdom) and the weeds (those outside the Kingdom) grow together until the harvest, when it would be obvious which was which.

The Net
All kinds of fish were dragged in together in the net, and only when it was pulled to shore were they separated into good fish (those belonging to the Kingdom) and bad (those not belonging).

Mustard Seed
The tiny seed growing to a huge tree indicates the sure, steady growth of the Kingdom.

Yeast
Similarly, the secret growth of the yeast hidden in the dough, shows that the work of the Kingdom goes on unseen.

The Treasure and The Pearl
These two parables show what value we should place on the Kingdom. Even though it may cost us everything we have to belong to Jesus, it would be worth every cent, every broken relationship.

In a person's lifetime, the ONE THING of vital importance is that he or she should accept Jesus Christ and so become a subject in the Kingdom of God.

* * *

When we pray, 'Thy Kingdom come', we acknowledge that there is a future aspect as well as a present one.

At the last supper, Jesus said, 'I will not drink again from the fruit of the vine until the Kingdom of God comes.'

Later, He said to those who arrested Him, 'My Kingdom is not of this world.'

And in Revelation, John heard a loud voice in Heaven saying, 'Now the salvation and the power, and the Kingdom of our God and the authority of His Christ have come. The Kingdom of the world has become the Kingdom of our Lord and of His Christ, and He will reign for ever and ever.'

* * *

Fill in page 5 now for Study 6.

STUDY 7

GIVING UP ... EVERYTHING

QUESTIONS

DAY 1   *Luke 13:1-9; John 9:1-3.*
a) What did Jesus teach the people, through the local news about the Galileans and the people of Siloam? How was this a warning to them?
b) Do you think the owner of the fig tree was unreasonable? sensible? cruel? spiteful? fair?

DAY 2   *Luke 13:10-21.*
a) How would you describe the attitude of the official of the synagogue?
b) Why did Jesus call him a hypocrite?

DAY 3   *Luke 13:22-30.*
a) Why did the people in Jesus' story expect to be allowed into the Kingdom?
b) For what reason do you expect to be admitted to Heaven?

DAY 4   *Luke 13:31-35.*
a) Why did Jesus not panic and run away when He got the message about Herod?
b) What was Jerusalem's reaction to Jesus' longing to love her?

DAY 5   *Luke 1:52-53; 14:1-14; 18:14.*
a) What is the main teaching of the parable Jesus tells here?
b) Discuss ways in which pride can creep into a Christian's life today.

DAY 6   *Luke 14:15-24.*
a) In this parable, who does the man giving the feast represent?
b) And the people who made excuses? And the people who came?
c) What does this show us about our priorities? Now read verses 23-24 again, and also John 3:18-19 and notice how the teaching is similar.

DAY 7   *Luke 14:25-35; John 12:24-26.*
a) What does Jesus say is necessary for anyone who wants to be His disciple?
b) Share some way in which you have had to face the cost of discipleship in your own life.

NOTES

GIVE UP ... YOUR SINS
Jesus' answer to the people in chapter 13:3 came straight to the point, and told them what they needed to know.

'Was God punishing the Galileans because of some great sin in their lives?' they asked.

'No,' said Jesus, 'but it's more important for you to get rid of the sin in your own lives. Repentance is essential for a right relationship with God.'

GIVE UP... YOUR LEGALISTIC ATTITUDE
The rulers of the synagogue had developed their own attitude to the Law, regarding it as a moral strait-jacket instead of a signpost pointing to the way of life that pleases God. Jesus showed that there would have to be a change of mind if these people were to enter the kingdom. The woman, who recognised her need, was made straight – the Pharisees remained crooked.

GIVE UP ... YOUR OWN IDEAS OF HOW TO BE SAVED
The actual number of people to be saved was a theoretical question often discussed by the Rabbis. Yet Jesus deems this unimportant, ignores the question and gets right to the heart of the matter. What does God say? That's the only question of any importance, for we can only enter the kingdom on His terms.

GIVE UP ... YOUR UNWILLINGNESS
Jesus was willing to put His life completely in His Father's hands and do His will whatever the cost. Jerusalem, however, had repeatedly refused God's offer of salvation and was unwilling to come and be loved by Him. Because of this, she signed her own death-warrant.

GIVE UP ... YOUR PRIDE
There is no place for pride or self-seeking in the Christian's life. Pride says, 'Me first –' 'I'm better than the other fellow.' 'Well, I really deserve the best....' etc.

Notice that Jesus is not here giving rules of etiquette for a party (how trivial that would be!) but He is using this parable to illustrate the spiritual truth of 14:11.

GIVE UP ... YOUR EXCUSES
How pathetic were the excuses of the men in the story! They wouldn't hold water for a minute. But how about your own life? Don't you make excuses to God? He can always see through them, of course.

This section should challenge you to review your priorities in life. The Lord Jesus has invited you to belong to Him, to put Him first in your life. But to be invited is not enough. One must accept.

GIVE UP ... EVERYTHING
Look back over the six previous headings we have just considered. Now we come to the one that strips away the last scraps of self that we love to cling to.

Jesus warns us that following Him could mean separation from those we cherish most, if our relationship with them interferes with loyalty to Jesus. Often loyalty to Jesus and natural affection within the family go hand in hand – for the gospel enriches human love – but where there is conflict, the claims of Jesus upon His follower must come first.

Building a tower is a costly business,
waging a war is dangerous,
and the follower of Jesus must be willing to face both costliness
and danger for His sake.

Are you willing?
Are you ready to lay every precious thing before Him and say, 'Take it, Lord, if need be'?
When you go home today, think over what Jesus has said in this study, and use this prayer if you can pray it sincerely:

'Lord, I make a full surrender,
All, I yield to Thee;
For Thy love so great and tender,
Asks the gift of me.'

* * *

Are you remembering to fill in the blank space on page 5?

STUDY 8
LOST AND FOUND

QUESTIONS

DAY 1 *Luke 15:1-10.*
a) What prompted Jesus to tell the stories of the lost sheep and the lost coin?
b) What main message was Jesus giving through these parables?

DAY 2 *Luke 15:11-24.*
a) In what way or ways was the younger son 'lost' (v. 32)?
b) What do you think is the most important verse in this story?

DAY 3 *Luke 15:25-32.*
a) Discuss the attitude of the older son. Was it: unkind? understandable? loving? fair? the way you would have felt?
b) How did this whole parable apply to the people in verses 1-2?

DAY 4 *Luke 16:1-8.*
a) Why did the dishonest manager 'fiddle' the books and reduce the debts people owed his master?
b) Think of a present-day example where a bad person has done something bad – but has done it well!

DAY 5 *Matthew 25:14-23; Luke 16:9-13.*
a) What reason is given here for why we should be careful how we use our money?
b) Which master (Luke 16:13) do you serve? How is your service reflected in your daily living?

DAY 6 *1 Samuel 16:7; Proverbs 21:2; Luke 16:14-18.*
a) Think of an example to illustrate the truth of Luke 16 verse 15 (second part).
b) How do today's verses back up Jesus' statement in Matthew 5:17?

DAY 7 *Luke 16:19-31.*
a) How does the title of this week's study apply to this parable?
b) What strikes you most forcibly in this story?

NOTES

LOST AND FOUND

LOST small white sheep, last seen near the flock mid-afternoon.

LOST Tuesday, one silver coin. Sentimental value.

LOST 'Prodigal', missing now for 3 years. Please contact father if you read this. Past wrongs will be forgiven and forgotten. Come home.

LOST men and women, boys and girls– some of whom have wandered off on their own because they couldn't care less about Jesus Christ, some have never heard of Him, and some have deliberately rejected Him and turned their backs on God.

Take a look at the '*LOST and FOUND*' column in your local newspaper. Behind every '*LOST*' notice there is a story of sorrow and disappointment, possibly heartbreak.

In our column above, the first three are sad, certainly, but the fourth is tragic, because it is true and because so many of these will be lost, not only in this life, but for all eternity.

The stories Jesus told certainly catch our imagination and we can identify with the people who have lost things, sharing their joy when the lost is found. But these delightful stories only touch the surface, and the teaching behind them goes ever so much deeper.

The Shepherd in the story was inconvenienced, anxious, tired, possibly cut or scratched – but when Jesus left the glories of Heaven and came into our sordid world to look for the lost, He was beaten and humiliated, tortured in body and soul, and it cost Him His life.

The Coin lay in a dark corner, lifeless, lost unable to help itself in any way. People who are separated from God are spiritually dead – but God cares about them. The woman found the coin, but it remained a coin.

'But God's mercy is so abundant and His love for us is so great, that while we were spiritually dead in our disobedience, He brought us to life with Christ. It is by God's grace that you have been saved' (Eph. 2:4 and 5).

The son who was separated from his father had gone away deliberately. It took a long time for him to come to his senses and admit that he was a failure at running his own life. So often it is pride which keeps people from experiencing the love of God. How crazy can you get?

The Father in the story waited ... ready to forgive at the first sign of the young man's return. God does much more than wait. God the Son, goes out to look for the lost ones, God the Spirit gives life to those who cannot help themselves, and God the Father receives repentant sinners into His arms of love, ensuring their salvation for all eternity. There is, indeed, joy in heaven over every sinner who repents.

* * *

The parable of the dishonest manager presents difficulties. How is it to be interpreted? Perhaps it will help if we remember that Jesus' parables:

l) were told in terms of everyday life that His listeners could identify with.

2) usually set forth one main point of spiritual truth.

The tax collectors and other outcasts (see ch. 15:1) were among the disciples in the audience. So it would seem that Jesus chose to wrap up His teaching in a story about a man just like them! And although this man was far from perfect, the one thing for which he was commended was that he used his opportunities there and then to prepare for his future life (when he would be dismissed).

The exact opposite is shown in the story of the rich man, and the point is more obvious. He did not use his opportunities while he had them, and he did not prepare for his future life (after death).

Let's pick up our newspaper, *THE LUKE TIMES*, again.

FUNERAL NOTICE

MANN Friends and relatives and important men of the town are invited to attend respectfully the public funeral of the late Mr Rich Mann, which will be held in the Splendid Parlour in his Summer Mansion. Flowers should be sent early in the day, as a great many wreaths are expected, and servants will be in attendance to arrange them in the Ballroom Beautiful. After the funeral, a grand banquet will be held, given by the deceased's father and five brothers. Strictly by invitation only.

And if we could be quite reverently fanciful for a moment, we might imagine an insert in *THE HEAVENLY HERALD* as follows:

'Angels, archangels, and all the company of Heaven are invited to a feast of great rejoicing for our beloved brother Lazarus, who will very soon enter into the joy of his Lord. His place is reserved beside Abraham. The singers and musicians will play the great 'Welcome Home' song as he arrives. The Spirit and the Bride say, 'Come'. 'Praise be to God!'

In the light of Jesus' parable, which party would you prefer to attend?

* * *

Thank God for the special thing He has taught you today,
and make a note of it on page 5.

STUDY 9

IF YOU HAD BEEN THERE ...

QUESTIONS

It would be a good idea to read the notes alongside each day's questions this week.

DAY 1 *Matthew 6:14-15; Luke 17:1-19; 2 Corinthians 2:10-11.*
a) What can you discover about forgiveness in these readings?
b) The Samaritan who was healed showed his gratitude by praising and thanking Jesus. What can you praise and thank Him for today?

DAY 2 *Luke 17:20-37.*
a) What does Jesus tell His disciples about Himself here?
b) How would you explain verse 33 (Mark 8:34-38 and John 12:23-26 may help you)?

DAY 3 *Luke 11:13; 18:1-14.*
a) Why did Jesus tell the parable of the judge and the widow?
b) Why, do you think, does God despise a proud and haughty self-concept so much?

DAY 4 *Luke 18:15-34.*
a) Discuss what childlike qualities are necessary for entry into the Kingdom.
b) What did the rich man think would win him eternal life? (Read Phil. 3:7-9 to see how wrong he was!)

DAY 5 *Mark 10:46; Luke 18:35–19:10.*
a) What things resulted from blind Bartimaeus being given his sight?
b) What were the attitudes of the onlookers in Luke 18:39 and 19:7?

DAY 6 *Luke 19:11-27.*
a) Why did Jesus tell this parable?
b) What were the servants told to do while the master was away (v. 13)?
c) Why were the first and second servants commended?

DAY 7 *Luke 19:28-44.*
a) How is Luke 18:31 a commentary on the Palm Sunday story? (Read 2 Kings 9:13; Ps. 118:26; Zech. 9:9; 14:4a, and Hab. 2:11.)
b) What was the reason Jesus gave for the future destruction of Jerusalem?

NOTES

'What a privilege,' we might think, 'to gather around Jesus in those days of long ago, and actually hear His teaching and His stories from His own lips!' If you had been there, hearing all this for the first time, how would you have responded to His teaching?

1. *Chapter 17:1-19.*
He gave four points about daily living.

 1) Don't cause anyone else to sin.
 2) Never refuse to forgive.
 3) Have real, genuine faith.
 4) Be humble – remember you are a servant of God.

You weren't there at that time, but over the past weeks you have been privileged to study what Jesus said in Luke's gospel. How have you been responding? Like the nine lepers who took it all for granted? or like the one who came back to Jesus and said 'thank you'?

2. *Chapter 17:20-37.*
The coming of the Kingdom of God was (strange though it may seem to us) a much discussed topic among the Jews.
   The Pharisees could not see that God's Kingdom had been revealed already in Jesus (see Notes on Study 6).
   The disciples had accepted this truth, and were ready for the further teaching on the Second Coming, which would be visible.
   If you had been there, would you have been prepared to believe everything that Jesus said?

3. *Chapter 18:1-14.*
Many books have been written on the subject of prayer, but here in two stories Jesus pinpoints the two most important aspects of it.
   The American Indians have a proverb: 'To learn to climb mountains, climb mountains; to learn to cross rivers, cross rivers.' Jesus says, in effect, 'To learn to pray, pray.'
   Point 1 – *Practise constant contact with God,* as this widow did with the wicked and self-centred man who was her judge. The judge does not represent God in this parable, but he is one of those, 'How much more –?' teaching aids, where Jesus shows that God's character is infinitely superior to that of fallen man.
   Point 2 – *Humble yourself as you stand before God.* A man's attitude to his God is all-important, as he comes to Him in prayer. How vividly the parable of the Pharisees and the Publican demonstrates this!
   If you had been there, would your conscience have been pricked?

4. *Chapter 18:15-34.*
Luke is careful in the arrangement of his book. Remember he said he was writing 'an orderly account' (Luke 1:3). He now contrasts the attitude of a child with that of a man who clings to

his earthly possessions. How clearly we can see the difference! Which one are you most like?

5. *Chapter 18:35 – Chapter 19:10.*
Bartimaeus and Zacchaeus. Two outcasts of society – though for different reasons. How would you feel if one or other came to join your church fellowship? What would you do about it? Jesus saw that each of them had a great need, the need of a Saviour. And that's why He came – to save the lost.

6. *Chapter 19:11-27.*
If you had been there, listening to the story of the gold coins, would you have picked up the point Jesus was making? As you neared Jerusalem, you might have thrilled with anticipation – perhaps Jesus was going to declare His Kingdom in the city, there and then! But by means of this parable, you would realise that there was to be a long period of waiting before the Kingdom would come in all its glory. You, as a servant of the King, would have to continue His work in the midst of those who said, 'We don't want this Man to reign over us.'

7. *Chapter 19:28-44.*
Imagine seeing the events of Palm Sunday as they were actually happening! Would you have known your Bible (Old Testament) well enough to see that here was prophecy being fulfilled before your eyes? Here is the King, the Messiah ... there is Royal David's city, waiting for Him.
But what's He doing? Why is He weeping?
Jerusalem had forfeited the privilege of being the city of King Jesus. It is not over her that He will reign. But God's plan is that He should be King over all nations, as Zechariah foretold: 'The Lord will be King over all the earth' (Zech. 14:9).
If you had been there ... would you have bowed humbly before Him, and acknowledged Him as *your* King?

* * *

Now fill in the space on page 5.

STUDY 10
HEAD-ON COLLISIONS

QUESTIONS

DAY 1 *Luke 19:45-48; 20:1; 21:5, 6, 37, 38.*
a) Where is the stage set for this week's study?
b) Why did Jesus call it 'a den of thieves' (see Mark 11:15, 16)?
c) What was the attitude of the common people to Jesus at this time?

DAY 2 *Isaiah 5:1-7; Luke 20:1-18.*
a) The Jews would realise that the vineyard in the story represented something. What was it?
b) Discuss who the various characters represented.
c) Why were the people so incredulous in Luke 20 verse 16?

DAY 3 *Luke 20:19-26.*
a) Imagine you are one of the Chief Priests. Write down what you would be thinking in verses 19 and 20.
b) How can Jesus' advice in verse 25 be applied to us today?

DAY 4 *Luke 20:27-44; Acts 4:1-3; 23:6-10.*
a) What can you learn about life after death from Jesus' words?
b) What proof does He give that there IS life after death? Can you think of any other proofs?

DAY 5 *Luke 20:45–21:4.*
a) Think of the best word you can to describe the teachers of the Law (Scribes).
b) In what ways was the widow in contrast to the teachers of the Law?

DAY 6 *Luke 21:5-24.*
a) What things does Jesus say in this passage which would encourage His disciples?
b) Jerusalem was attacked and destroyed in 70 AD. What did Jesus advise His followers should do at that time?
c) What can we discover about Jesus from today's reading (see also Luke 18:31-34)?

DAY 7 *Luke 21:25-38; 2 Peter 3:10-13.*
a) We live in the age between the fulfilment of the prophecy we read about yesterday, and the one we read about today. What directions are given in these verses to guide us in our daily living?
b) How would you answer someone who said to you, 'Our world has gone crazy, it's out of control. Where's it all heading, anyway?'

NOTES

In our remaining three studies, we shall try to discover what key thoughts Luke had in mind when he compiled his account of the last days of Jesus on earth. Why did he include some incidents and omit others? In this week's study he paints a picture of the gathering storm. The authorities have had enough of this disturbing preacher from Galilee, but it proves more difficult than they realise to get rid of Him.

The 'head-on collisions' take place in the Temple in Jerusalem – the one place above all others where God and man can come together. Ideally they should have met in harmony, with humility on man's part and covenant love on God's. But there is something terribly wrong on man's side, and Jesus takes drastic measures to expose it.

ATTACK NO. 1
By a mighty, action-packed 'Visual Aid', Jesus shows up the pretence and corruption of those who traffic in the sacred place.

COUNTER-ATTACK
Can't you imagine the hurt pride, the indignant self-righteousness of the chief priests, teachers of the Law, and elders as they demand from Jesus what right He has to speak the way He does? How wisely He handles them!

ATTACK NO. 2
Jesus actually answers their question in the parable of the vineyard. It is all too clear to those listening, that He is the 'dear Son' of the story, and He knows exactly what is in their hearts. Hurt pride turns to rage – but His time has not yet come.

COUNTER-ATTACK
A trap, this time. How innocent it looks! But Luke is careful to show that no trap is clever enough to catch the divine Son of God – rather, Jesus is able to turn the question to give some basic teaching.

ANOTHER ATTACK – FROM THE OPPOSITION
Their religion consists of half-truths about Scripture (and how often we meet people like that). But they have chosen the wrong person to try to confuse! He Who is the Truth, cannot but show them that they are merely parading their own ignorance.

ATTACK NO. 3
By producing a real teaser from the Scriptures relating to David (their revered ancestor), Jesus shows that He can outwit them at their own game. He then warns His disciples, in front of everyone else, about the supposedly religious people, and He contrasts them with a poor widow who is demonstrating her genuine devotion to God.

The friction recorded by Luke thus far has served to show that the Jewish religion of that day was full of man-made customs and false beliefs, which could not co-exist with true faith. Not only would the Temple building be destroyed some 40 years later, but what it stood for would also have to be cleared out, as the pure light of Christianity flooded in. The head-on collision between Jesus and the corrupt system had to come, so that wrong religion would be shown up for what it was.

The section ends with a looking forward to that great Day when Jesus will come again in power and glory. God will dwell with redeemed mankind and live among them, and there will be no temple any more, because the Lord God Almighty and the Lamb will be in the midst.

* * *

The Holy Spirit is your teacher.
Write today's 'lesson' He has taught you on page 5.

STUDY 11
'THERE WAS NO OTHER GOOD ENOUGH ...'

QUESTIONS

DAY 1   *Exodus 12:1-14; Luke 22:1-6.*
a) What did the Passover commemorate?
b) Who do you think was responsible for Jesus' death?

DAY 2   *Luke 22:7-23.*
a) Only Peter and John were allowed to know where they would eat the Passover meal. Why do you think it was kept so secret?
b) What things did Jesus say at supper which indicate that He knew exactly what was ahead?

DAY 3   *Luke 22:24-38.*
a) How did Jesus show His disciples –
   that His Kingdom is not like any earthly Kingdom?
   that the old order of Judaism is to be replaced by the Church?
b) What was it that foiled Satan's plan to get Simon?

DAY 4   *Luke 22:39-53.*
a) What was Jesus' main concern for (1) Himself?; (2) His disciples?
b) What shows that Jesus submitted voluntarily to the powers of darkness?

DAY 5   *Luke 22:54-71.*
a) When the Lord turned and looked at Peter, what did Peter remember?
b) What else could he have remembered which would have helped him?
c) The Jewish Council sat in judgement on the prisoner. What was the statement which condemned Him? Who was really being judged (see John 3:18)?

DAY 6   *Luke 23:1-12.*
a) What charges about Jesus did the Council bring before Pilate? (Compare this with yesterday's reading.)
b) What was Herod's attitude to Jesus? And Jesus' attitude to Herod?

DAY 7   *Luke 23:13-25.*
a) What was Pilate's verdict on the prisoner? How many times does he say this?
b) Look up Matthew 27:4 and 1 Peter 2:22. What do these readings tell us? Who then, was guilty?

NOTES

In his book 'The Saviour of the World', Michael Wilcock, with fascinating insight into this section, gives a clear picture of what was happening in the chapter entitled 'Satan's Hour'.

Satan had a plan – a plan of destruction

The occasion: Passover time. It couldn't be put off any longer.

The organisers: The official representatives of Judaism, the rulers of Israel.

The betrayer: Satan had his man, Judas.

Everything is prepared. The Mastermind behind it makes sure nothing will go wrong ... and nothing does.

God had a plan – a plan of salvation

The occasion: Passover time. Planned since the time of Moses, when deliverance from bondage was assured by the blood of a lamb.

The organisers: The official representatives of Judaism, the rulers of Israel. They were unwittingly being used by God as the human framework for His Son's atoning death.

The betrayer: There had to be somebody (that was part of the plan). And Judas now sells his soul to Satan.

Jesus told His disciples, 'Go and prepare...', but everything was already prepared, more fully than they realised.

* * *

God needed a lamb, a lamb to take away the sin of the world. There was no other good enough, than the One who took the bread and said,

'This is My body, broken for you,' then took the cup and said, 'This is My blood, poured out for you.'

* * *

In the Garden of Gethsemane, Jesus could see these two plans converging. Think what it meant to Him. It was far more than foreknowledge of a humiliating and excruciatingly painful death that He had to endure. He clearly saw all the forces of evil, empowered by His arch-enemy Satan, bringing their wicked schemes to bear upon Him, to gain a supernatural victory over Him.

Could they break down His perfect record of sinlessness?

Could they divert Him from obedience to His Father's will?

Could they torture Him spiritually beyond His endurance?

He saw also, in the midst of the physical suffering that lay ahead, that dreaded moment when the sins of the whole world would be laid on Him, and even His Father would turn away His face

> 'O make me understand it,
> Help me to take it in,
> What it meant to Thee, the Holy One,
> To bear away my sin.'

Surely, this must be one of the most sacred passages in God's Word:

'Father, if you are willing, take this cup from Me....'

What agony could be greater than this? No wonder His sweat was like great drops of blood. 'Father, take away this cup....'
And then ... victory!

'Not my will, but Thine be done.'

And an angel appeared and strengthened Him.
In this moment of extreme crisis – JESUS HAD TRIUMPHED! All that followed was the outworking of that triumph.

* * *

One event followed another, but Jesus was calm, and in control of Himself and the situation. He was innocent (how the Bible underlines this fact!), no-one could find any trace of guilt in Him; He is the perfect, sinless Lamb of God. This suffering was His Father's will, it was the cup that His Father had given Him.
At every point, His enemies were playing into His hands to accomplish God's great plan of salvation for mankind.

* * *

Do you still need to be reminded about page 5?

STUDY 12
THE END – AND THE BEGINNING

QUESTIONS

DAY 1 *Luke 23:26-34.*
a) Why did Jesus tell the women what He did in verse 28?
b) What did Jesus ask for those who crucified Him? Why do you think He did so?

DAY 2 *Luke 23:35-43.*
a) What derogatory comments were shouted at Jesus while He was on the cross? Who said them?
b) What did the thief's request in verse 42 show? What did Jesus offer him?

DAY 3 *Matthew 27:50-53; Luke 23:44-56.*
a) What unusual happenings accompanied the death of Christ?
b) Read Matthew 27:57-60 and John 19:38-39. What can you discover about Joseph of Arimathea?

DAY 4 *Luke 18:31-34; 24:1-12.*
a) What two important things did the angels have to tell the women?
b) What was the difference between the way the women received the message and the way the apostles did?

DAY 5 *Luke 24:13-35.*
a) Cleopas and his friend knew what many people today know about Jesus (read again vv. 19-24). What, then, was missing that they were so unhappy?
b) How was the Word of God the answer to their problem?
c) Discuss whether or not this is true for people today.

DAY 6 *Luke 24:33-49.*
a) List the different feelings shown by the friends of Jesus in this passage. What did Jesus wish for them when He appeared (v. 36)?
b) Upon what does Jesus focus their attention?

DAY 7 *Luke 24:45-53.*
a) What four guidelines – which also apply to the Church today – did Jesus give His disciples?
b) Share something precious you have learned from Luke's Gospel.

NOTES

THE END

On the Cross, Jesus' last triumphant cry was, 'It Is finished!' (John 19:30). The work that the Father had sent Him to earth to accomplish was completed.

Think back over our studies in Luke:

He had spoken with authority,
He had trained His disciples,
He had taught about the Kingdom of God,
He had lived in perfect obedience to the Father,

and now He had drunk to the dregs, the cup of suffering for sin.

THE BEGINNING

Very early in the morning, at the very beginning of a new day, at the beginning of a new week, the women went to the tomb.

But Jesus had gone!
Risen!

Can't you feel the excitement?

Before dawn, while everything was dark, the Son of God burst forth, creating a new beginning. The light of the glorious Gospel of Christ would be shed over all the world by the power of the Holy Spirit. No wonder the two angels appeared to the women 'so bright that their eyes were dazzled!'

A new day, a new era, had dawned.

* * *

THE END

– That's what it seemed like to the women who came to anoint a dead body.
– That's what it seemed like to Cleopas and his friend as they walked the weary miles home.
– That's what is seemed like to the disciples, shivering with fright, behind locked doors.

But it was really –

THE BEGINNING

– of a new purpose (v. 47)
– of a new home (v. 49)
– of a new joy (v. 52)
– of a new life (v. 53)

No wonder Paul writes:

42

'If Christ has not been raised, then your faith is a delusion and you are still in your sins' (I Cor. 15:17).

Remember why Luke wrote this book?
He did it so that his friend, Theophilus, would know the full truth about Jesus Christ.
Have you a friend who does not know that Jesus came to save him? Someone who doesn't realise that Christ died to take away his sin? Remember, Jesus is 'THE WORLD'S ONLY HOPE.'
Luke wrote 'an orderly account' of it all. You might find it easier to chat to your friend at work, invite him home for a meal, or lend him a Christian book. But each of us who loves the Lord has the responsibility of sharing the Good News with our friends. For this is the only way that 'the message about repentance and forgiveness of sins' can be 'proclaimed to all nations', as our Lord Jesus commanded.
What are YOU going to do about it?

* * *

Look at all you have written on page 5.
Praise God for all you have learned.

ANSWER GUIDE

The following pages contain an Answer Guide. It is recommended that answers to the questions be attempted before turning to this guide. It is only a guide and the answers given should not be treated as exhaustive.

GUIDE TO INTRODUCTORY STUDY

Leaders, it is suggested that YOU start the ball rolling by sharing with your group some, or all, of what is set out below. PLEASE DON'T just read it to them, but try to tell it in an interesting way.

'Soon after Jesus returned to heaven, His disciples began the task of spreading the good news of the salvation which He had brought. They started in Jerusalem itself and thousands were converted. From Jerusalem the gospel spread to neighbouring provinces, then to countries beyond, until Christianity had been firmly established in western Asia and eastern Europe. This growth took place over a period of about 30 years (from the AD 30's to the 60's) and is recorded in the Book of Acts.

'Those who became Christians were immediately taught the stories and teachings of Jesus. This emphasis on the life of Jesus was one reason why it was essential that the 12 apostles should be men who had been with Jesus from the time of His baptism to the time of His ascension (Acts 1:21), so that they could give eyewitness accounts of what He had said and done. These 12 apostles carefully instructed the believers, who memorized the stories and sayings of Jesus, and then went out to spread the news to others. New converts were taught similarly, and they, too, went out teaching and making disciples of others. In this way the teaching spread.

'As the Church grew, the original eyewitnesses of what Jesus had said and done became more and more scattered. Some went to far countries, some died, and some were killed by the enemies of Christianity. In order to preserve the teachings which had been handed down from these men, certain written collections of the sayings and deeds of Jesus began to appear. Here we see the origins of our four Gospels, the first of which was probably written about AD 60, and the last about AD 90. It is difficult to speak with certainty on the time and writing of each of these books, but from evidence within the writings themselves, together with references to them by non-Biblical writers of the time, we may suggest the following as a possible explanation of the reason for four separate Gospels.

'Some time between AD 55 and 60 (that is, before Paul had gone to Rome), Peter visited Rome with Mark as his helper, and taught the Roman Christians concerning Christ. When Peter left Rome, Mark stayed behind, and the Roman Christians asked Mark to write down the story of Jesus as they had heard it from Peter. This Mark did, and the result was Mark's Gospel.

'Soon after, Paul arrived in Rome as a prisoner with Luke and Aristarchus, and was held prisoner in Rome for 2 years. Mark, who was still in Rome, got to know Luke very well as both of them stayed with Paul for some time (Col. 4:10, 14; Philem. 24). Over the years, Luke had been collecting and preparing materials for the books he himself had been planning to write, and on arrival in Rome was pleased to find Mark's completed record. He was able to take some of Mark's material and include it in his own writings. The first part, which covered the period of time up to the ascension of Christ, we know as the Gospel of Luke. The second part is called the Acts of the Apostles.

'Luke was a Greek and thereby the only writer of the New Testament who was not a Jew. He was not a disciple during the time of Jesus, and was probably converted during Paul's second missionary journey. By his use of the word 'we' in his Acts narrative (Acts 16:6-11, etc.), we know that he went with Paul's party to Philippi, where he probably stayed when the rest of the party moved on (Acts 17:1). It was several years later that he rejoined Paul on his way to Jerusalem (Acts 20:1-6). He was with Paul both in Jerusalem and throughout his two year imprisonment in Caesarea (Acts 24:27), and then went with Paul to Rome (Acts 27:1; 28:16), where he remained with him through another two year imprisonment (Acts 28:30). He quite possibly remained with Paul for the rest of the apostle's life, and was the only one with Paul during his final imprisonment in Rome (2 Tim. 4:11). As well as being a doctor (Col. 4:14) Luke was an accurate historian, who dated Bible events according to secular history.'

Quoted from – *THE NEW TESTAMENT SPEAKS* by D. C. Fleming.

'SOMETHING TO REMEMBER' – Page 3

Leaders, it is your responsibility to encourage your group members to look out for something from each study that they can note down on page 3. It is amazing how much more people will remember, if they come to God's Word in a spirit of expectancy.

Use the prayer provided BEFORE you begin the study together each week.

* * *

Decide now if you cannot fit in all 12 studies. If you have to leave out one (or even two) studies, omit either Study 6, 7 or 8 – but on no account leave out Studies 11 and 12.

* * *

In preparation of these studies, I have leaned heavily on Michael Wilcock's book, *THE MESSAGE OF LUKE, The Saviour of the World* (Pub. IVP in the series, 'The Bible Speaks Today'). Although it is more expensive than most paperbacks, it is well worth the money, and you would appreciate it for a deeper study of Luke's Gospel.

GUIDE TO STUDY 1

DAY 1
a) He would be one of God's great men. He would be filled with the Holy Spirit from birth. He would bring many people back to the Lord. He would prepare the people for the Messiah. (Note references to the Holy Spirit in this chapter.)
b) He became unable to speak.

DAY 2
a) He would be great and the Son of God. His kingdom would never end.
b) The Holy Spirit would come upon her, and the power of God rest upon her.
c) One of humble submission and acceptance.

DAY 3
a) The baby leaped in her womb, and she was filled with the Holy Spirit.
b) God's mercy extends to those who reverence God (v. 50), it was shown to Abraham and his descendants (v. 55).
God's power had done great things for Mary (v. 49), had scattered the proud (v. 51) and brought down kings (v. 52).

DAY 4
a) He wrote 'His name is John'; he got back his speech; he praised God; he was filled with the Holy Spirit; he spoke God's message.
b) Jesus.
c) John (his own son).

DAY 5
a) Personal.
b) God.

DAY 6
a) The Holy Spirit was with Simeon, He had shown Simeon that he would see the Messiah before he died, and the Holy Spirit had impelled him to go to the Temple that day.
b) Probably the fact that he said Jesus would be a light to the Gentiles.

DAY 7
a) Listening to the teachers, asking them questions and giving answers.
b) That He identified with God as His Father (rather than Joseph) and that He had come to do His Father's work.

GUIDE TO STUDY 2

DAY 1
a) The word of God came to him.
b) 'A voice'. ('Someone shouting' GNB.)
c) He was to prepare the way for the Lord.

DAY 2
a) Prove by the way you live that you really have repented.
Give to the poor if you have more than you need.

Don't collect more than is legal.
Don't steal or accuse falsely. Be content with your pay.
b) Personal. (This answer should pinpoint something in your own life that needs to be changed.)

DAY 3 a) He chose (of His own free will) to identify with all mankind, even though He had not sinned and had nothing of which to repent.
b) Psalm 2: He is the Son of God. Isaiah 42 : He is the Servant of the Lord.

DAY 4 a) To show that Jesus was of the royal line of David, that He was a true Jew and a 'son of Abraham', but also Son of God. In tracing Jesus' ancestry back to Adam, Luke shows that Jesus identified with Gentiles as well as Jews.
b) Sin and death came by Adam; forgiveness and eternal life by Jesus.

DAY 5 a) Because the devil knew He was hungry and to tempt Him to doubt His Father's faithfulness to provide.
b) By using words of Scripture.
c) We can do the same if we have learned the Scriptures. (These Bible Studies help us with this.)

DAY 6 a) That He was the One sent from God that the prophets foretold years before.
b) They were angry because He implied that God's message was not only for the Jews (in fact some Jews would even forfeit it) but for the Gentiles too.

DAY 7 a) As written in the different verses.
b) Six verses: Luke 3:22, 23, 38; 4:3, 9, 22.

GUIDE TO STUDY 3

DAY 1 a) His words, His teaching and His authority.
b) By His word.
c) To preach the good news of the kingdom of God in all the towns of that area.

DAY 2 a) To listen to the word of God.
b) The word of Jesus ('because you say ... ').
c) Personal.

DAY 3 a) Because, as a leper, he was not allowed to go near healthy people, let alone touch them. Think what it must have meant to him to feel a friendly touch.
b) The fact that Jesus told him his sins were forgiven.

DAY 4 a) Eating and drinking with notorious characters. Not fasting.
b) A doctor, because He came to heal the spiritually sick. A bridegroom,

because it was a joyful time when He was with people.

DAY 5   a) That it was a day to put God (and the Son of God) first, and to do good – rather than a day when people had to be ruled by the letter of the law.
b) Personal.

DAY 6   a) He spent the night out in the hills praying.
b) Apostles, disciples (or followers) – note, a large crowd of them – and a great number of people.
c) Belonging to the Kingdom of God and expecting a reward in heaven – rather than an easy life and riches now.

DAY 7   a) Personal.
b) The person who comes to Jesus, listens to His words, and puts them into practice (v. 47).
c) We have come, we have listened to His words in verses 27-38 – are we going to put them into practice?

GUIDE TO STUDY 4

DAY 1   a) That His word had authority, even over disease.
b) Disease.
c) That he, a Gentile, should have such great faith in Him.

DAY 2   a) The man who died was young and was the only son of a widow. (Widows were dependent on their sons or near relatives, had no legal rights, and could not receive any inheritance.)
b) Death.
c) Fear, and praise to God.

DAY 3   a) Baptise with the Holy Spirit, purge the evil from Judaism and 'burn with fire' (i.e. punish) those who would not repent.
b) It is reaching out to others in love – the blind see, etc. (Luke 7:22); spreading the good news of salvation (v. 22); it is much superior to anything which had ever been (v. 28; Rom. 14:17).

DAY 4   a) Tax collectors were outcasts, as this woman was, and she had the right response to Jesus; Simon was a Pharisee and his response was as described in verse 30.
b) Sin.
c) Personal.

DAY 5   a) The Twelve, some women who had been healed.
The secrets of the Kingdom of God.

b) How the word of God is received by people.
c) As 'the good soil' and 'mother and brothers' (v. 21).

DAY 6　a) That Jesus heard when they called for help, and that He was perfectly in control of the situation.
b) Shaken (by the brush with death in the storm) and now terrified by this maniac.
c) That although we are powerless, He is able to cope with anything. We need to trust ourselves completely to Him.

DAY 7　a) Suggestions – her personal meeting with Him was even more important than her healing; she would not feel ashamed; others would be ready to welcome her (as she had been 'unclean' before); perhaps also to put Peter in his place!
b) Six.
c) That Jesus can even take the sting out of death (I Cor. 15:55-57).

GUIDE TO STUDY 5

DAY 1　a) Preach the Kingdom of God, heal the sick and cast out demons.
b) Jesus gave them power and authority.
c) Discussion. (Points to bring out: the natural, human point of view – but hadn't they seen Jesus working miracles?; did Jesus really expect them to feed the crowd? Why did He say this? See John 6:6 etc.)

DAY 2　a) That He was the Messiah (Christ).
b) That He must suffer, be rejected and killed, and rise on the third day.
c) 'This is My Son whom I have chosen: listen to him.'

DAY 3　a) They were spiritually immature.
b) Personal.

DAY 4　a) They were reacting in a natural manner (revenge, tit-for-tat) rather than in Jesus' way of love.
b) Personal – put in your own words.

DAY 5　Pray for more workers.
Go to the towns where Jesus will go.
Stay in a house where you are welcomed.
Heal the sick.
Say, 'the Kingdom of God has come.'

DAY 6　a) They found that Jesus' name had power even over demons.
b) That our names are written in heaven.
c) That God had chosen 'the weak things of the world ...' (I Cor. 1:26-29).

DAY 7   a) Discussion. (Some thoughts: 'Love your neighbour' is a divine command, not an option. It can be a costly business – in time, effort and money. 'Loving' is active, not passive. God requires us to love those we don't like, even hate, and this is only possible by letting God love them through us).
b) That we must get our priorities right and not find we have no time to get to know Jesus more.

GUIDE TO STUDY 6

DAY 1   a) God is our Father; His Name is holy; He forgives sins; He will continually answer our prayers; He wants what is best for us and will give the Holy Spirit to those who ask.
b) We can talk to God as to a loving father; we should glorify Him first in our prayers, then bring our own requests. Prayer should be urgent and sincere, and we believe that He hears.

DAY 2   a) Satan and God.
b) To destroy the works of the devil, and to turn people from the power of Satan to God.

DAY 3   a) Jesus would die, and rise the third day.
b) For travelling so far to hear the wisdom of Solomon.

DAY 4   a) Ritual washings – unclean hearts; tithe – neglect justice; get seats of honour – are proud; appear religious – no compassion.
b) We should not do things in private that we would be ashamed of if they were made public.

DAY 5   a) Fear God (i.e. reverence His power and authority for judgement). Don't blaspheme against the Holy Spirit. (Leon Morris in the Tyndale Commentary says, 'We must understand this, not of the uttering of any form of words, but of the set of the life.... It is this continuing attitude that is the ultimate sin. God's power to forgive is not abated. But this kind of sinner no longer has the capacity to repent and believe' [p. 211]).
b) Personal.

DAY 6   a) Personal. (Suggestions – Be aware of the powerful influence material things have on our lives; realise that wanting more – which is quite natural – is a sin; check often the way we spend our time and money).
b) Devoting our time, talents and resources to the service of God.
They don't decrease, get stolen, or become destroyed.

DAY 7   a) We should be ready for Him at any time, and in the meantime live holy, godly lives.
b) Personal.

GUIDE TO STUDY 7

DAY 1
a) He taught that God does not punish sin by sending tragedy; God's wrath is on all sin. The warning was for them to turn from their sins.
b) Personal.

DAY 2
a) Critical, unfeeling (for the woman), evasive (getting at Jesus by addressing the woman) – etc.
b) Because he gave the impression of being righteous and good, but was totally lacking in love and concern for others.

DAY 3
a) Because they had eaten with Jesus and had heard his teachings they knew about Jesus. However Jesus never recognised them as His own, indicating that they had never obeyed His teachings and never knew Him personally.
b) Personal.
(Leaders, this second question is most important. Let your group give their honest personal answers, and then direct them to such Scriptures as John 1:10-12; John 3:5; John 14:6; and Acts 16:30, 31.)

DAY 4
a) Jesus came to do the Father's will, and He knew that God, who created Time, would plan His purposes exactly. (Note: 'the third day' is a poetic expression meaning at the time of completion).
b) She would not let Him.

DAY 5
a) It is that all pride, self-interest, concern for personal advantage, self-centredness, etc., must be given up by those who follow Christ.
b) Discussion.

DAY 6
a) God.
b) Those who reject His offer of salvation. Those who accept it.
c) That the most important thing in life is to be sure you belong to Jesus.
(Leaders, stress the fact that God's invitation of love is open to all, and those who do not respond condemn themselves).

DAY 7
a) He must put Jesus absolutely first in his life – before parents, husband/wife or children – and must die to himself and his own desires.
b) Personal.

GUIDE TO STUDY 8

DAY 1
a) The fact that the 'religious' men of the town were criticizing Him for befriending outcasts.
b) That God loves even the outcasts and the 'no-hopers', and wants them to love Him. (Some people may pick out other aspects of the story.)

DAY 2 a) He was not lost in the sense that he didn't know his way home, but as far as his father was concerned he was lost because the father didn't know where he was.
Because there was no contact between them, the father had lost a son.
b) Personal (v. 18? v. 24?).

DAY 3 a) Discussion.
b) The outcasts of society were like the younger son and Jesus longed for them to receive Him. The self-righteous ones were like the older brother and didn't want the others to be saved.

DAY 4 a) He wanted to buy the friendship of his master's debtors, so that in future he could look to them for help.
b) Personal.

DAY 5 a) The way we handle the money our Lord has given us on earth shows how fit we are to serve Him here, and in heaven (v. 11).
b) Personal.

DAY 6 a) Own ideas (e.g. huge buildings, worldly honour and glory, etc.).
b) Verse 17 shows that Jesus upheld the law. The Pharisees ruled by the letter of the law, but Jesus came to explain the principles behind it.
(Leaders, if your group is likely to query verse 18, on divorce, prepare yourself for this.)

DAY 7 a) The rich man was eternally lost, Lazarus had obviously been 'found' before he died.
b) Personal.

GUIDE TO STUDY 9

DAY 1 a) The one who seeks forgiveness must repent; we should never refuse to forgive; our forgiveness by God depends on our willingness to forgive others; Satan gets a wedge in if we are unforgiving.
b) Personal.

DAY 2 a) He will come again and reveal Himself; first He must suffer and be rejected. This principle is central to the teaching of the gospel.
b) Death to self and our own desires is the gateway to eternal life in Christ (see Rom. 6:6, etc.).

DAY 3 a) To teach His disciples that they should always pray and never become discouraged (v. 1).
b) Personal. (It is the opposite to admitting and confessing one's sin, which is vital for full dependence on God).

DAY 4	a) Discussion.
	b) Keeping the Law.

DAY 5	a) He followed Jesus; he gave thanks to God; the people in the crowd praised God.
	b) They tried to keep the blind man from Jesus; they resented Jesus going to the home of a tax-collector.

DAY 6	a) Because the people were expecting that Jesus would proclaim Himself king very soon (v. 11).
	b) Trade with the money (RSV and NEB); invest it (LB); see what they could earn (GNB); put the money to work (NIV).
	c) Because they had done exactly what the master had told them to.

DAY 7	a) The extra readings show how prophecy was actually being fulfilled.
	b) Jerusalem had rejected the opportunity God gave them and did not recognise Jesus when He came (v. 44).

GUIDE TO STUDY 10

DAY 1	a) In the Temple in Jerusalem.
	b) Because the merchants were buying and selling in the Temple, and robbing the people.
	c) They listened eagerly to Him.

DAY 2	a) The nation of Israel – God's people.
	b) The owner: God. The tenants: the leaders of Israel. The slaves: prophets. The owner's son: Jesus.
	c) Because they could not imagine that God's plan of redemption could be transferred to any other nation.

DAY 3	a) Personal. (Should include anger, rage, fear, planning to bribe men so as to trick Jesus.)
	b) It is right to give loyalty to the country one lives in (unless it conflicts with one's faith – see Acts 5:29), and also to contribute to the Lord's work.

DAY 4	a) Heaven will not be a mere continuation of this world; it is another, different world, which we are unable to understand at present. The redeemed will not marry, they will be like angels, they will never die. (Note: D. G. Miller adds that marriage is for: a. fulfilment of man's social needs, and b. the procreation of the race – neither of which will be necessary in Heaven.)
	b) Since those who belong to God are one with Him by faith, and since God cannot die, then those who are in Him are alive for ever.
	Personal.

LUKE • ANSWER GUIDE • • • • • •

DAY 5	a) Personal.
	b) Proud/humble. Showy/self-effacing. Rich/poor. Had plenty of money left/ had nothing left.
DAY 6	a) Verses 9, 13 (important), 14 & 15, 18 & 19.
	b) To leave the city and flee to the hills. (Note: When Jerusalem was attacked, the Christians did just this, but the Jews would not leave and perished with the city.)
	c) Jesus knew exactly what was in the future. (Note: He is the same today, and knows what is ahead.)
DAY 7	a) Verses 28, 34-36; 2 Peter 3:11.
	b) Personal answer based on these verses. God is in control.

GUIDE TO STUDY 11

DAY 1	a) The time when the Israelites, under Moses, left the slavery of Egypt and God brought them to freedom.
	b) From these verses one could say the chief priests, Judas, Satan. See notes for a more comprehensive answer. This will be discussed further in Day 7.
DAY 2	a) So that Judas would not betray Jesus before the appointed time, and before they had all had the meal together.
	b) He was to suffer (v. 15), He would not be with them much longer (vv. 16, 18), His body would be broken and His blood shed, He knew about the betrayer.
DAY 3	a) Verse 26.
	Verse 30.
	b) Jesus' prayers for him.
DAY 4	a) (1) That He should be strong enough to do His Father's will.
	(2) That they should pray, so that they would not fall into temptation.
	b) He went into the garden as usual, knowing what would happen (v. 39); He would not let His disciples defend Him (v. 51); He acknowledged His role in the drama at this point (v. 53).
DAY 5	a) Verse 61.
	b) Verse 32.
	c) The statement that He was the Son of God.
	The Council, who did not believe He was the Son of God.
DAY 6	a) That He encouraged the people not to pay their taxes to Caesar, and that He claimed to be a King.
	b) He wanted to see Him performing some miracles.

Jesus would not say a word.

DAY 7   a) That He was innocent. Three times.
b) That Jesus was innocent.
The final question is framed for discussion. Barabbas, the Jews, Pilate, Herod, Judas – these are starters and the discussion could continue to show that mankind – all of us – helped to put Jesus on the Cross because of our sin.

GUIDE TO STUDY 12

DAY 1   a) Jesus was going to be crucified – to bring Salvation to the world. But the people of Jerusalem had rejected Him, and again and again He had warned that there would be no salvation, no eternal life, for those who reject Him.
b) Forgiveness.
Encourage discussion, bringing out the fact that forgiveness is only possible through faith in the atoning death of Christ, and therefore, Jesus' prayer presupposed that these men would change their attitude and be 'born again'.

DAY 2   a) Verse 35 – the Jewish leaders; verses 36, 37 – the soldiers; verse 39 – one of the criminals.
b) It showed that he had repented of his sin and believed Jesus could save him. Jesus gave him eternal life.

DAY 3   a) Three hours of darkness; the curtain in the Temple was torn, top to bottom; the earth shook, rocks split, graves opened, people raised to life.
b) A secret follower of Jesus; asked Pilate for the body; friend of Nicodemus; he was rich and laid Jesus in his own new tomb.

DAY 4   a) Jesus was risen; remember what He said.
b) The women remembered His words and were prepared to believe, but the apostles didn't believe them.

DAY 5   a) A personal encounter with the Lord Jesus.
b) Jesus spoke to them through the Scriptures to show them God's plan for the world (which was not what they had expected).
c) Discussion.

DAY 6   a) Excitement, terror, unbelief, joy, amazement. Peace!
b) The Scriptures.

DAY 7   a) Biblical Theology (v. 46); Evangelism (v. 47); Apostolic Authority (v. 48, may be expressed in simpler terms); Spiritual Dynamic (v. 49).
b) Personal.

THE WORD WORLDWIDE

We first heard of WORD WORLDWIDE over 20 years ago when Marie Dinnen, its founder, shared excitedly about the wonderful way ministry to one needy woman had exploded to touch many lives. It was great to see the Word of God being made central in the lives of thousands of men and women, then to witness the life-changing results of them applying the Word to their circumstances. Over the years the vision for WORD WORLDWIDE has not dimmed in the hearts of those who are involved in this ministry. God is still at work through His Word and in today's self-seeking society, the Word is even more relevant to those who desire true meaning and purpose in life. WORD WORLDWIDE is a ministry of WEC International, an interdenominational missionary society, whose sole purpose is to see Christ known, loved and worshipped by all, particularly those who have yet to hear of His wonderful name. This ministry is a vital part of our work and we warmly recommend the WORD WORLDWIDE 'Geared for Growth' Bible studies to you. We know that as you study His Word you will be enriched in your personal walk with Christ. It is our hope that as you are blessed through these studies, you will find opportunities to help others discover a personal relationship with Jesus. As a mission we would encourage you to work with us to make Christ known to the ends of the earth.

Stewart and Jean Moulds – British Directors, **WEC International**.

A full list of over 50 'Geared for Growth' studies can be obtained from:

ENGLAND   *North East/South:* John and Ann Edwards
5 Louvaine Terrace, Hetton-le-Hole, Tyne & Wear, DH5 9PP
Tel. 0191 5262803 Email: rhysjohn.edwards@virgin.net
North West/Midlands: Anne Jenkins
Tel. 01524 734797 Email: anne@jenkins.abelgratis.com
West: Pam Riches Tel. 01594 834241

IRELAND   Steffney Preston
33 Harcourts Hill, Portadown, Craigavon, N. Ireland, BT62 3RE
Tel. 028 3833 7844 Email: sa.preston@talk21.com

SCOTLAND   Margaret Halliday
10 Douglas Drive, Newton Mearns, Glasgow, G77 6HR
Tel. 0141 639 8695 Email: mhalliday@onetel.net.uk

WALES   William and Eirian Edwards
Penlan Uchaf, Carmarthen Road, Kidwelly, Carms., SA17 5AF
Tel. 01554 890423 Email: penlanuchaf@fwi.co.uk

UK CO-ORDINATOR
Anne Jenkins
2 Windermere Road, Carnforth, Lancs., LA5 9AR
Tel. 01524 734797 Email: anne@jenkins.abelgratis.com

UK Website: www.wordworldwide.org.uk